Original title:
The Vine's Voice

Copyright © 2025 Creative Arts Management OÜ
All rights reserved.

Author: Mariana Leclair
ISBN HARDBACK: 978-1-80567-066-7
ISBN PAPERBACK: 978-1-80567-146-6

Serenade of the Entwined

In tangled arms, they sway and dance,
With leaves that giggle, a leafy prance.
They whisper secrets, oh so sly,
As clueless critters scurry by.

A squirrel stops, then bursts in glee,
"Is that a joke?" he asks the tree.
The branches chuckle, bending low,
"Just hanging out, putting on a show!"

Whispers in the Garden Shade

Beneath the boughs, the laughter grows,
A ladybug joins for comedy shows.
"Why did the cabbage turn red?" it teases,
"Because it saw the salad dressing!" it sneezes.

The daisies giggle, sharing their puns,
While the sun chuckles, sending out runs.
In this green realm, all woes take flight,
Translated tales make the garden bright.

Ballad of the Swaying Boughs

The branches swing in playful jest,
As robins chirp, they never rest.
"What's the best drink?" the willow quips,
"Root beer, because of our leafy tips!"

With every sway, they crack a joke,
The oak joins in, a merry bloke.
Laughter rings, a sylvan parade,
Even the dandelions join in the charade.

Rhythms of the Climbing Shadows

As sunlight dances on the fence,
The shadows twirl, making no sense.
"I'm tired of being just a shade,"
Says one old vine, with a wink made.

The others chuckle, in leafy heat,
"Let's form a band, we can't be beat!"
A comedy club? Oh what a dream,
Where every twist is more than it seems.

Arboreal Cadence

In the forest, branches sway,
Squirrels dance in grand ballet.
Birds tweet jokes about their flight,
Leaves chuckle in the morning light.

Rabbits hop in rhythm's tease,
Bumblebees hum with such ease.
Each vine twirls with a goofy grin,
Nature's party is about to begin!

Roots gossip 'neath the soil's cloak,
While mushrooms crack the best of jokes.
A caterpillar joins the fun,
To the beat of the warming sun.

In this world of green delight,
Laughter echoes, day and night.
Every twist and every vine,
Brings a joy that's simply divine!

Tales from the Ancient Boughs

In a tree where wise ones chatter,
Old branches share their silliest matter.
A acorn claims to be a king,
While moss rolls up to laugh and sing.

Beetles boast of their grand plans,
While ants form tiny marching bands.
The bark whispers secrets loud,
Urging leaves to gather 'round the crowd.

A spider weaves a tale so sweet,
Of how she always skips a beat.
The breeze joins in with a puff and sigh,
As butterflies waltz by on the sly.

In this leafy world, so absurd,
Every branch has truly heard.
With wisecracks that boldly grow,
Nature, it seems, steals the show!

The Lilt of the Climbing Flora

Vines frolic as they climb so high,
Humming tunes that never die.
With every twist, they twist the laugh,
In the garden's quirky photograph.

Petals cheer as wind plays games,
Tickling leaves with delicate names.
A sunflower winks with a proud glow,
While daisies giggle below in row.

As the climbers stretch and sway,
Their giggles chase the clouds away.
A pebble rolls with a wink and joke,
A rock's punchline always evokes.

Laughter rings through nature's hall,
In every chirp, there's a playful call.
In this world, a vine's wise jest,
Brings humor to the evergreen fest!

Secrets of the Overgrown

Whispers of the thicket dwell,
In ketchup vines, stories swell.
A fern tells of a rusty fence,
While ivy masks its own suspense.

Crickets chirp a witty tune,
Beneath the rays of the mocking moon.
And every blade of grass participates,
In making fun of the lazy mates.

Roses wear their thorns with pride,
While tulips tease, they won't abide.
Composting leaves hoot with glee,
As nature's show unfolds with glee.

Every nook has tales to spare,
In a garden's laugh, troubles wear.
Among the weeds and nature's spree,
Lies a secret of comedy!

Secrets Wrapped in Green

In the garden, whispers sprout,
Grapes gossip as they pout.
"Did you hear what happened here?"
"Someone's drinking far too near!"

Leaves wear hats of shady greens,
While reds and purples share their beans.
"My juice is sweeter, I can boast!"
"But I can give you Sunday toast!"

Harmony of the Leafy Veil

Underneath the leafy shade,
Laughter in the branches played.
"Can you pass the sunlight, friend?"
"No way! You'll cause a grape to bend!"

Swaying vines dance with delight,
Tickling bees that take their flight.
"Let's form a band, a music crew!"
"Only if we can find a brew!"

The Language of Twine

Tangled words between the spree,
Vines chat in a sassy glee.
"How do you do?" "Oh, quite fine!"
"Care for a twist over some wine?"

Jokes exchanged upon the breeze,
"Your curves are quite the sight, oh please!"
"Just watch your step on this fine grind,
Or you might trip and rewine!"

Chords of the Woodland

In the woods, the chords resound,
Merriment all around.
Trees giggle, bending low,
"Hey there buddy, take it slow!"

With each strum, the branches shake,
Berries bounce with every quake.
"Let's sing a song, the night is long!
I'll bring the snacks, you bring the song!"

Gentle Songs of the Overgrowth

In the garden, whispers creep,
Telling secrets plants can't keep.
A sunflower wearing shades, so neat,
Winks at ants on tiny feet.

A leaf sings high, a twig sings low,
While sneaky snails steal the show.
Frogs join in with ribbits bold,
As daisies sashay, proud and gold.

Tangles of Memory and Harmony

Vines wrap round the old oak tree,
Making shapes, like glee-filled spree.
A squirrel hops, trying to sway,
While blooms giggle in bright display.

Old memories stuck in the ruck,
Tangled tales of luck and pluck.
A dandelion, puffed with pride,
Dreams of flight, with laughter tied.

The Nature's Enchanted Dialogues

Breezes chat with flowers bright,
Shuffling petals, pure delight.
A bee buzzes, then makes a toast,
To the bug that thinks it's a ghost!

The weathered branch hums a tune,
As puddles dance beneath the moon.
With every rustle, the woods engage,
In chorus, life's a funny stage.

Weaving Dreams in the Wilderness

Spider webs glimmer with delight,
As fireflies flicker in the night.
A hedgehog dons a tiny hat,
While thinking he could really chat!

The whispers in thickets case the scene,
A raccoon plotting with the unseen.
Giggling mushrooms, little and spry,
Converse with shadows, oh so sly!

Murmurs from the Verdant Embrace

In the garden, whispers play,
A grape's joke on a sunny day,
"Why did the berry cross the road?"
"To vine and chase the beetle's code!"

Leaves giggle, swaying to the tune,
Bumblebees buzz, planning a boon,
"What's a grape's mission? To have some fun!"
"Munching sunlight, till day is done!"

Songs of the Twisted Stems

Twisted stems hum a quirky song,
Pulling each other along,
"Did you hear about the lazy leaf?"
"He fell asleep, oh what a relief!"

Ripe fingers tap a bouncy beat,
As tendrils dance in the summer heat,
"Why did the cluster wear a frown?"
"A berry told him not to clown!"

Lament of the Winding Roots

Roots grumble beneath the earth's crust,
Twisting about, it's a must,
"Why can't we ever just relax?"
"Because we're tangled in crazy tracks!"

Tapping the soil, they jest and jive,
"Why don't we start a roots' archive?"
"To tell tales of our silly strife,"
"And share the depth of our plant life!"

Harmony in the Canopy

Up high, branches sway and laugh,
Birds join in on nature's half,
"What do you call a bird in a vine?"
"A feathered friend seeking something fine!"

A squirrel chirps from the leafy loft,
"My acorn coffee is so soft!"
"Why do they invite the leaves to play?"
"Because they know how to sway all day!"

Arboreal Whispers

Leaves gossip in the breeze,
Telling tales of playful bees.
Roots have punchlines underground,
While branches chuckle all around.

Squirrels dance on limbs up high,
Cracking jokes about the sky.
Bark has puns that make us grin,
Nature's humor wears a sin.

Nature's Gentle Refrain

The bushes snicker at the grass,
While flowers giggle as they pass.
Pinecones roll and laugh with glee,
Nature's jesters wild and free.

Birds perform their silly songs,
With melodies that feel like prongs.
The sunbeams wink and tease the shade,
Creating pranks that won't soon fade.

Winding Stories of the Wild

Roots twist tales both bold and bright,
Of critters sneaking in the night.
A raccoon wears a mask so sly,
While fireflies flicker, oh so spry.

Fungi giggle at passing feet,
With wise jokes that can't be beat.
In the thicket, laughter's heard,
Each snicker shared, a tiny word.

Ciphers of the Ceaseless Grove

The trees are scribes with leafy pens,
Writing stories where laughter begins.
Branches bent in fits of cheer,
Whispering jokes for all to hear.

A rabbit chuckles with delight,
While ants debate who's got more bite.
The creek is laughing as it flows,
With secrets that only nature knows.

The Poetry of Green and Gold

In the garden, laughter sprouts,
Green jokes hide between the clouts.
Sunlight dances on the wine,
While grapes giggle, quite divine.

With cheeky roots beneath the ground,
They whisper secrets, humor found.
Tiny leaves in playful chats,
Play tag with bugs, oh silly spats!

A playful breeze knocks hats askew,
As colors laugh in every hue.
The nectar drips in merry streams,
Tickling taste buds, sweetened dreams.

Nature's jesters in rows align,
Wearing crowns of twisted vine.
Each sip a chuckle, each taste a grin,
In this jest, the joy begins!

Melodies of the Leafy Realm

In the wood where whispers twine,
Leaves frolic, dress up fine.
Squirrels tap dance, oh what glee,
In this leafy jubilee.

Chirps and chuckles fill the air,
Hopping grasshoppers with flair.
They form bands, a merry crew,
Singing songs of fresh dew.

Creeping vines with wiggly ways,
Join the fun in leafy plays.
Each bend a laugh, each twist a tease,
Nature's pranks are sure to please.

Beneath the sun, all join the rhyme,
Life's a melody, sweet as thyme.
So raise a toast to nature's whims,
In this realm, the laughter brims!

Chords of Nature's Symphony

A plucky string, a leafy tune,
Even mushrooms dance by moon.
With bouncy beats of crickets' play,
They turn the night to a cabaret.

Whispering winds in playful sighs,
Make the daisies roll their eyes.
They sway and twist, a giggly song,
In their world, nothing's wrong.

Acorn bells ring, to laughter, they cling,
As branches bop, and bramble springs.
Joyful birds in cheeky flight,
Strike up the chords of pure delight.

When nature plays, the heart takes wing,
Listen close, oh listen, sing!
In every rustle, every noise,
There's music made of nature's joys!

Creating Connections in Bloom

Each petal flutters with a wink,
Pink and yellow make you think.
Butterflies with giggly grins,
Join the party; let's begin!

Budding friends in every hue,
With daffodils, we'll dance anew.
Roses share their scented jokes,
As bees buzz in with happy pokes.

They twirl and swirl in vibrant glee,
Making friends beneath the tree.
Nature's joke book, filled with laughs,
Grows lush in this garden's paths.

So sip the nectar, taste the fun,
In every bloom, a smile's spun.
Together, roots intertwine and play,
Creating joy in a floral display!

Whispered Prophecies of the Grove

In the grove, leaves chatter away,
Guessing secrets they can't say.
A squirrel nods, with acorn in hand,
"I heard the tree's got a big old plan!"

Roots gossip low, tickling the ground,
While birds hold court, circling around.
"Did you see that branch? It nearly fell!"
"Oh, hush! They'll talk! Just pick up a shell!"

Lyrical Echoes of the Undergrowth

In the shadows, fungi hum a tune,
Crooning softly beneath the moon.
"Hey, did you smell that? It's quite divine!"
"Of course, it's from that last fine wine!"

The critters all gather, sharing a laugh,
Debating the best spots for sunlit bath.
A rabbit hops in with a carrot so bold,
"Let's toast our tales; they never grow old!"

Conversations in the Canopy

High in the branches, chatter and cheer,
As winged voices echo, spreading good cheer.
"Did you see that owl? He's such a tease!"
"Yeah, and the sloth still snoozes with ease!"

Parrots squawk loud, tales of food trade,
While the youth of the forest parade.
"Who knew that tree was quite so ripe?"
"The berries are better; they've got more hype!"

The Nestled Narratives of Nature

In the thicket, tales weave and loom,
With spiders crafting stories in the gloom.
"Did you hear of that bear? Quite the dancer!"
"Yeah, but his moves lack real romance, sir!"

A hedgehog pipes up with a prickly wink,
"Dance like the flowers; give them a wink!"
Nature chuckles, her voice so sweet,
"Every creature here has got tales to repeat!"

Aria of the Hidden Clusters

In the garden, whispers creep,
Grapes giggle soft, secrets deep.
Beneath the leaves, they plot and chat,
Wondering who will taste them fat.

Vines twist in a playful dance,
Tickling bees in a clumsy prance.
"Oh, what a bunch!" the birds would sing,
As squirrels debate the best of bling.

Laughter echoes in the daylight,
While sunlight glimmers, shining bright.
Each berry dreams of juice so sweet,
While ants march by on tiny feet.

Beneath the sun, the joy is raw,
"We're the stars!" they shout with glee and awe.
In the twilight, they laugh and boast,
For tomorrow, they'll be loved the most.

Verses from the Clinging Sages

Among the vines, wise words collide,
Nature's jesters with nothing to hide.
They flutter tales from branch to bark,
Sharing gossip till dusk turns dark.

One vine calls, "I'm the best in town!"
While others giggle, wearing a crown.
"Look at me, ready for the feast!"
As rabbits plan a grape-filled feast.

A butterfly joins the fun and flair,
Deciding which cluster can best compare.
With every twist, a giggle grows,
In the shadows, a wise vine knows.

In this vineyard, we laugh so free,
To drink from joy is the key, you see!
As clinging sages spread their cheer,
Nature's fun is forever near.

Tales in the Shade of Growth

Under leaves, secrets unspool,
Young sprouts play, keeping it cool.
"I'm taller!" one boasted with flair,
While others whispered, "Not if we dare!"

The wise old grapelet grinned with pride,
"I once rolled downhill, what a ride!"
The young ones chuckled, "Sounds quite bold!"
As morning dew began to unfold.

"Who's the juiciest?" one teased with zest,
While ladybugs pondered, they felt blessed.
Each twist tangled in stories grand,
In every leaf, laughter takes a stand.

As shadows danced in the golden sun,
All gathered 'round, a picnic begun.
In this warm shade, joy takes root,
In the tales of growth, no one stays mute.

Echoes of the Nature's Embrace

In the orchard, laughter spills,
Where vines climb high with playful thrills.
"Who's the juiciest?" a grapelet cries,
As bumblebees buzz and butterflies fly.

Across the rows, friendships bloom,
While sunbeams break through the leafy room.
Grapes cling together, a merry band,
Telling tales that grow on every strand.

"Look over there, a cluster of fun!"
As critters gather to bask in the sun.
With every rustle, stories ignite,
In this embrace, everything feels right.

As folk arrive with baskets wide,
The laughter swells, no need to hide.
For in this spot, under the trees,
Nature sings with the sweetest breeze.

Chime of the Growing World

In the garden, things get silly,
Tomatoes giggle, oh so frilly.
Lettuce winks beneath the sun,
Radishes dance, they're having fun.

A carrot whispered, 'Let's play tag!'
While cucumbers wore a leafy rag.
Peppers joked with a spicy tease,
As flowers swayed in the gentle breeze.

The beans were swinging on a vine,
While pumpkins chatted, sipping wine.
'Who knew the soil could be so bright?'
Chiming laughter echoed through the night.

Sonnet of the Verdant Whispers

The broccoli rolled its tiny eyes,
As spinach accused it of being sly.
A radish burst out with a big surprise,
Saying, 'Friends, we broccoli cannot lie!'

The peas were plotting a grand parade,
While onions cried, 'Why can't I play too?'
Amidst the greens, plans were made,
To have a feast in the dew-kissed hue.

Let's not forget the garlic's bold stance,
'I'm pungent, but let's enjoy this chance!'
Under the sun, what a wild dance,
As veggies frolicked in pure romance.

Whispers Through the Canopy

Leaves are chattering, what a treat,
Squirrels gossip while they eat.
The branches sway to a funny song,
As sunlight spills where it belongs.

A frog croaks out a little tune,
While fireflies twirl around the moon.
Mushrooms giggle beneath the trees,
While bumblebees mime, with the greatest ease.

The dandelions shout, 'We're the stars!'
While owls contemplate their little wars.
Nature's circus, what a delight,
As whispers play in the soft moonlight.

Tendrils of Secrets

In the garden where mischief brews,
Cabbages wearing tiny shoes.
With tendrils pointing, they conspire,
'Let's play tricks that never tire!'

Radicals of radishes roll with glee,
Causing ruckus, what a sight to see!
The herbs are whispering crafty plots,
'Tomorrow's stew will hit the spots!'

Pumpkin declared, 'I'm the king today!'
While parsley danced and led the way.
A silly leaf said, 'Don't mind me,
Just leaf it all to destiny!'

Reverie of the Lush Labyrinth

In the garden, plants gossip loud,
Cucumbers joke, making the carrots proud.
Roses flirt with bees, oh what a sight,
While cabbages dance, beneath the moonlight.

Trees chuckle softly, sharing their tales,
Of mischievous squirrels and windblown gales.
The daisies giggle, dressed in white,
While wildflowers twirl, pure delight.

A lettuce whispers, 'Life's a big play,'
'Always green, yet we wilt anyway!'
Tomatoes boast, 'We ripen with grace!'
Who knew such veggies could win a race?

So gather round if you wish to hear,
The secrets from branches, loud and clear.
In this lush maze, where laughter grows,
Nature's humor in sunshine flows!

Dialogue of the Nature's Veils

In the shade of leaves, the chatter flies,
As butterflies boast of their blue skies.
The ferns whisper back, 'Oh, what a show!'
While the beetles debate the best way to glow.

Breezes swirl in a playful dance,
Tickling the petals, in a merry trance.
The stones look on, as wise as they are,
Thinking, 'These plants have gone quite bizarre!'

Grass blades tease the ants, 'Slow down, please!'
While owls mock, 'You'll never catch that breeze!'
And vines, they wriggle with glee, oh my!
Singing sweet sonnets under the sky.

Such banter flows like a river of cheer,
With each new season, more tales appear.
Nature loves laughter, the world is her stage,
An endless performance, no need for a cage!

Rhapsody of the Leafy Aria

Once in a forest where giggles grew,
The trees played drums, a greenish hue.
The mushrooms chimed in, with a flouncy hip,
As the vines swung low, doing their flip.

A squirrel composed a symphony bright,
With acorns and twigs, it was sheer delight.
While the brook babbled secrets of old,
Sharing whispers of stories untold.

Plants put on hats, for an evening feast,
The daisies served beans, as each sought a beast.
The thorns wore tuxedos, looking so grand,
While petals performed, across sun-soaked land.

In this symphony, oh what a jest,
Nature's own orchestra, always the best.
With laughter and joy, they sing in the sun,
The leafy delight, oh what fun we've begun!

Sagas of the Spiraling Green

In a garden tale where oddities thrive,
The zucchini plays king, taking a dive.
The radishes jest, 'We're roots of the fun!'
While tomatoes compete for the brightest red sun.

The spinach proclaims, 'I'm the best of greens!'
While peas laugh aloud, weaving silky sheens.
A broccoli bard strums his flute with flair,
While herbs join in song, swirling in air.

Ducklings parade through the garden of cheer,
With beetroot in tow, they twirl and they leer.
The cabbages croon in their leafy cabaret,
As the sun dips low, claiming the day.

So heed the whispers from seeds far and wide,
Each leaf has its story, no need to hide.
In this spiraling realm, where humor plays keen,
Lies laughter, the magic, in every green scene!

Voices Beneath the Arbor

Underneath the leafy shade,
The squirrels start a charade,
They chatter loud, a comical sound,
While acorns tumble to the ground.

A snail gives a slow parade,
With tiny friends who join the raid,
They joke about the rain today,
'At least it's not a sunny fray!'

Beneath the branches, shadows dance,
While bees all buzz and prance,
The leaves whisper, 'Don't fall behind!',
As a branch teases with a gentle grind.

Frogs croak tales of distant lands,
While ants prepare their tiny bands,
In this green realm, it's quite a hoot,
Where nature's jokes are absolute!

Narrative of the Verdant Veins

Among the roots, the whispers weave,
As greens conspire, make you believe,
That daisies wear the finest hats,
And earthworms share the latest chats.

Each blade of grass has tales to tell,
Of grasshoppers who dance so well,
While dandelions puff and sigh,
'Don't pluck us! We're your alibi!'

The ivy creeps with a cheeky grin,
Telling secrets where they've been,
While mushrooms laugh in little packs,
And hold their meetings at the cracks.

A robin sings, 'I'm not a crow!'
With every hip-hop, to and fro,
In this green booth of endless pranks,
Nature's humor fills the banks!

Waltz of the Gnarled Grasses

In fields where the tall grasses sway,
They twirl and twist in a funny way,
With breezy giggles swirling around,
A dance-off starts without a sound.

Ladybugs wear their party attire,
Inviting all to the grassy choir,
A beetle rolls in with flair,
"Anyone need a chauffeur's dare?"

The elder tree throws shade so grand,
While owls wink from their lofty stand,
"Don't leaf me hanging!" the branches shout,
As wildflowers roam and scout about.

A caterpillar dreams of its flight,
"I'll be a butterfly tonight!"
With all the laughter from the ground,
In this wild waltz, joy is found!

Soliloquy of the Flourishing Foliage

The leaves gossip in a playful way,
Sharing tales of yesterday,
"Did you hear what the breeze did say?
It tickled my toes, oh what a day!"

A sunflower stands with cheeky pride,
"I'm the tallest!" it beams wide,
While the ferns flip their little fans,
"Tall tales from a lady in strands!"

The thorns whisper a secret cheer,
"Prickly charm brings the bugs near!"
Bumblebees drone with grinning glee,
"Stop and smell the sweet brie!"

In this green stage, all play their part,
With laughter for the weary heart,
Nature's comedy, a lively spree,
Where every leaf is full of glee!

Serenades of the Silent Woods

In the woods where whispers play,
The bushes giggle, come what may.
A squirrel jokes about the breeze,
While trees nod, dressed like a tease.

A rabbit trips, does a little dance,
He grins wide, must have taken a chance.
The owls hoot in comical shrieks,
As they plot with the cheeky peaks.

The mushrooms chuckle, stacked so high,
With tiny caps that wink and sigh.
The ferns sway to the forest's tune,
These antics will make you laugh till noon.

Each leaf rustles, a raucous cheer,
In silent woods, there's fun to spear.
A hidden jest in every nook,
Nature's humor in every look.

Secrets of the Green Realm

In a garden where gnomes pretend,
The flowers gossip, around the bend.
A sunflower sways, takes a bow,
While garden bugs giggle, oh wow!

The carrots wear hats, made of clay,
While cabbage roles in a playful fray.
The bees hum tunes, sweet and light,
In secret chats till the fall of night.

A stubborn weed tries to impress,
But all it does is cause a mess.
The gardener slips, lands on his seat,
While roses chuckle at his defeat.

Underneath the olive tree shade,
Lies the laughter of greenery made.
Each leaf a witness to nature's spree,
In this realm of joy, we're all so free.

Ballads of the Boughs

Up high on branches, laughter grows,
With acorns chuckling, row by rows.
The wind carries tales, a funny jest,
As the robins chirp their very best.

Squirrels wear hats made of bark,
Planning antics till it's dark.
While the leaves join in with a sway,
Nature's band plays all day.

A woodpecker knocks with style so bold,
Making music as stories unfold.
The branches creak, they join the fun,
In this airy place where all is one.

Each twiggish hug is a giddy spree,
With every rustling, pure jubilee.
Nature's laughter, a sweet, light sound,
In the ballads that dance all around.

Tales of Unseen Connections

Beneath the soil, roots hold a chat,
Exchanging jokes while wanting to sprat.
Earthworms twist with glee so sly,
While moles just giggle as they pass by.

A patch of moss claims it's an art,
Creating carpets that steal the heart.
The ants march forth, a tiny parade,
With humor hidden in every trade.

A creeping vine tries to catch a laugh,
Tickling leaves with a gentle half.
The dewdrops giggle, glistening bright,
Sharing secrets by morning light.

Each connection whispers funny tales,
Through thickets and woods, laughter prevails.
In nature's network, jokes intertwine,
A joyful world, where all align.

Melodies in the Breeze

A grape swung low, it had a sway,
Singing to the sun, all day.
'Twist and shout,' it cheered so loud,
While bugs danced round, all very proud.

With every breeze, a new refrain,
Voices mingled, joy like champagne.
The pumpkins laughed, they rolled around,
While daisies giggled, on green ground.

In this place of youthful cheer,
Even the carrots would volunteer.
They formed a band, a merry crew,
Chasing shadows, with a view.

Each leaf a dancer, each fruit a star,
Pitched a tune, near and far.
The sun took note, with rays so bright,
As laughter echoed, day and night.

Unraveling the Green Tendrils

Oh those tendrils, curling fine,
Spinning tales of summer wine.
Tickling frogs in leafy beds,
They whisper secrets, softly spread.

A ladybug upon a leaf,
Declared the vine, a comic thief.
With every twist and turn they played,
A rollicking puppet, unafraid.

Bees buzzing tunes, what a sound,
Plucking notes from underground.
The earthworms cheered, they swept the floor,
As roots took bows, seeking encore.

In the tangle, chaos blooms,
With giggles trapped in nature's rooms.
Twisting vines sing light and free,
Moments caught in nature's spree.

The Silhouette's Serenade

In twilight hues, the shadows prance,
While vines perform their evening dance.
Bestowing hugs on trees so tall,
They sway and tangle, no need to call.

A ghostly leaf, a starry laugh,
Whispers secrets, on a path.
The moonlight chuckles, in delight,
As branches play tag, through the night.

With shadows cast upon the ground,
They giggle in the silence found.
A frog joins in, with ribbits rare,
A symphony beneath the air.

Sunset sings, the vines applaud,
Their playful jigs, a little flawed.
In nature's stage, they twirl in joy,
As shadows wink, each girl and boy.

Beneath the Leafy Canopy

Under leaves, a party sprung,
The fruit was ripe, a song was sung.
Lemonade rivers flowing near,
Every sip brought shouts of cheer.

Mice played cards, a shocking bluff,
While squirrels squabbled, 'This is tough!'
Beneath the branches, worries flew,
A picnic spread for everyone, too.

With whispers shared from flower to vine,
A gather of laughter, so divine.
The mushrooms giggled at every joke,
As fireflies danced, with a sparkle and poke.

In this oasis of leafy bounds,
Joy sneaks in with chuckling sounds.
Under the sky, so bright and green,
Life's funny moments, a true routine.

Nature's Gentle Murmur

In the garden, whispers play,
Plants giggle at the sun's bright ray.
Bees do a dance, oh so absurd,
They buzz like they've just heard a word.

Worms wiggle, wearing tiny shoes,
Critics of the grass that they peruse.
Leaves clink cups in a leafy brawl,
Nature's laughter echoes through it all.

Echoes of the Twisting Roots

Roots rapped up in a twisty song,
Bouncing to a beat that's all wrong.
They trip and tangle, what a sight,
Planning a dance in the pale moonlight.

Squirrels chirp, keeping the tempo,
While ants strut, dressed up in retro.
The ground giggles, a secret shared,
Life's a comedy if you've dared.

Song of the Climbing Shadows

Shadows stretch and begin to tease,
Tickling the trunks of tall, proud trees.
Lizards laugh in a sun-kissed spree,
While crickets join in, so carefree.

Branches wave, a silly ballet,
As flowers nod in a bright display.
They're all in on the joke, it seems,
As the breeze carries their funny dreams.

Grapes of Silent Stories

Grapes hang low, with a secret grin,
Winking at the sun, letting fun begin.
They whisper tales of past delight,
Of summer parties that last all night.

Their laughter bubbles, a fruity sound,
As they plot to tumble to the ground.
Each bounce and roll is a comic scene,
Making jam out of life's routine.

The Lyric of Elastic Tales

In a garden where whispers bounce,
Beneath the sun, they twist and flounce.
A grape said, 'Tell me, what's the deal?
When you squish my juice, how do you feel?'

The leaves giggled, 'We're not just for snacks,
Without us, the fruit would fade, and that lacks.
For every sip that you take with cheer,
Just remember, we whispered out here!'

A snail cruised by in a grape-leaf car,
He sighed, 'Life's a race; I'm not getting far!'
But the branches swayed, 'Oh snail, hold tight!
Your shell's a mansion, your future's bright!'

Then came the beetle, dancing with flair,
'I'm the DJ of leaves, with beats to spare!'
The vines laughed loud, 'Just keep it low,
Save the wild moves for after the show!'

Intricate Patterns of Growth

Underneath the sky so blue,
The shoots are plotting a dance or two.
'What's this tango?' the roots chime in,
'Every wiggle brings a burst of win!'

The sunbeams laughed, 'Oh what a sight,
A conga line of greens, pure delight!'
'Watch your step, dear vine, not too much twist,
Or you might find yourself in the mist!'

The little bugs threw a leafy ball,
'Join us, dear plants, let's have a ball!
With pollen confetti, we'll dance with glee,
Who knew life could be so carefree?'

As raindrops dripped, they sang a song,
'Nature's a circus, and we belong!
So lift those tendrils, let laughter sprout,
With every chuckle, there's joy about!'

The Voice of Verdant Dreams

In a realm where laughter grows on trees,
The flowers chatter with buzzing bees.
'Oh dear dew, why are you so bright?
Because I woke up to a sun-filled night!'

The branches sighed, 'Life's a quirky show,
With each twist and shout, we steal the glow!'
The grass joined in, a carpet of cheer,
'Who knew being verdant would bring such a sphere?'

The breeze chimed in, a playful tease,
'You're all great, but I'm the main squeeze!'
And so they danced, in a grand soirée,
With roots to ground them, they'll sway away!

So here's to the green in whimsical jest,
Where even a cactus can wear a fest!
Life's not so serious, just let it flow,
With each little giggle, let the joy grow!'

Tales Woven in Nature's Loom

In a tapestry of green that twirls,
Every petal's laugh is a secret world.
'Hey, twig, do you have a story to share?'
'Only that I dodged a bird in mid-air!'

The soil chuckled, 'I'm the best friend,
Feeding the vines as they twist and bend.
Without my hugs, where would you be?
Just a stranded sprout, sipping on dreams!'

The sunbeams winked, 'Look at you all,
In this wild party, you're having a ball!'
The clouds added fluff, a comfy embrace,
Wrapping the green in a soft, warm case.

So here's to the tales that nature unfolds,
With giggles and grins, as the story's told.
For laughter and growth go hand in hand,
In this whimsical, verdant wonderland!'

Twisting Echoes of the Canopy

In a dance with the breeze, they sway and twirl,
Leaves gossip softly, like a leafy girl.
They tickle the branches, giggling all day,
As shadows are cast in a silly ballet.

Rope-like and winding, they cling with a grin,
Whispering secrets of where they have been.
Each twist has a tale, with punchlines galore,
A punchline of photosynthesis, oh what a chore!

The sun shines on gossip, they bask in the light,
Mimicking chatter, they sing through the night.
With roots in the soil, they tell wild tales,
Of insects and critters and singing snails.

So next time you wander beneath their wide sway,
Imagine the jokes that these branches convey.
For nature's a stage, and the laughs will unfold,
In the echoes of foliage, a comedy gold.

The Embrace of Earth and Sky

From the soil, they leap with a joyous shout,
Entwined in the laughter that no one can doubt.
They stretch to the heavens with whimsical flair,
Debating the colors of clouds in midair.

With roots so deep, they crack up the ground,
While swirling above, making silly sounds.
The wind plays conductor, waves arms in delight,
As branches respond like they're ready to fight.

They tickle the stars, asking for a dance,
While insects below just can't miss the chance.
"I can shimmy," says one, "while you do the twist!"
A performance so grand, it can't be missed.

So gather 'round nature's odd stage set,
Where earth hugs the sky, with no hint of regret.
For humor abounds in each leafy embrace,
In a world full of giggles, there's always a place.

Whispers of the Climbing Vine

Upward they scramble, a curious crew,
Trading wisecracks like a cartoon zoo.
Each twist of their bodies, a pun to impart,
As they reach for the sun, with a viney heart.

"Do you hear that?" one quips, in a leafy tone,
"It's the sound of our friends, but we're not alone!"
Bantering back and forth in the canopy shade,
While squirrels roll their eyes at the jokes that they've made.

A tumble of laughter, a sprawl of green glee,
The leaves share a secret, "It's clearly just me!"
And as thunder rolls in, they giggle and tease,
Summoning storms like it's just a breeze.

With a pixie-like charm, each vine speaks its truth,
In playful parables recalling their youth.
The earth shakes its head at their vine-tangled quest,
In whispers and chuckles, they're truly the best.

Growing Tales of Resilience

Small sprouts begin with a flicker of jest,
Determined to grow, they put laughter to test.
"Nobody can stop us!" they shout with a cheer,
As they stretch out their limbs, planting joy without fear.

Facing the rain with a comical grin,
Bouncing on raindrops, they welcome the din.
"We're here for the party," they sing with delight,
As storms drum a rhythm that keeps spirits bright.

In gardens of struggle, they find humor's way,
Abundant in fails, yet they never dismay.
With roots in the chaos, they rise above strife,
Turning mishaps to tales of a raucous life.

So as they keep growing, through sun and through gloom,

They share with the world their resilient bloom.
In whispers of laughter, their stories entwine,
A frolicsome journey on the path to divine.

The Interlaced Chronicles

In a garden bustling with glee,
Grapes tell jokes without decree.
The tomatoes rolling with laughter,
Say, "This is like the funniest chapter!"

Carrots chime in, they can't contain,
"Why did the cucumber dance in the rain?"
Because he knew that in life, oh dear,
Every drop is a chance for a cheer!

The leafy greens giggle and sway,
Whispering secrets of yesterday.
A mischievous carrot does a cartwheel,
While radishes wonder who stole their meal!

As the sun sets sharing its glow,
They swear they saw a potato show.
With punchlines sprouting from root to bud,
Their laughter echoes, stirring the mud.

The Fusion of Root and Sky

Up high, the sky waves to the dirt,
"Hey root, are you tired or just inert?"
The roots chuckle, "We're digging down deep,
While you float around, what a piece of a heap!"

The clouds roll in, full of puffy pride,
"You roots need a vacation! Come up for a ride!"
But the roots scream back, "No way, José,
It's comfy down here with our earth buffet!"

The sun jumps in, with a wink and a grin,
"Let's all get together, let the fun begin!"
They blend like a smoothie, a light-hearted mix,
"Who knew our connection would taste so unique?"

The laughter rings out through the branches around,
As roots and clouds share their joy unbound.
In this wild union of earth and the sky,
Always remember, it's fun that'll fly!

Enigmas of the Leafy Labyrinth

Wander through greens where riddles unwind,
Each leaf whispers mysteries, one of a kind.
"Why did the beetroot wear a disguise?"
A kale leaf chuckles, "To hide its surprise!"

In the maze of lettuce, so crisp and so bright,
A broccoli stands, trying to take flight.
"What's green and feels like it's got no cheer?"
"A sad little pea, stuck without a dear!"

Chasing shadows, they giggle and quake,
"What's a grape's favorite dance? The grapevine shake!"
With all of their humor, they twirl 'round and sway,
This leafy adventure brightens the day.

As night starts to fall on this whimsical scene,
They dream of adventures, both funny and keen.
So if you find greens with a joyful refrain,
Just stop for a moment - laughter shall reign!

The Choir of Green Existence

In a garden where chirps meet the clover,
Plants form a choir, getting bolder and bolder.
"What's a plant's favorite song?" starts the lime,
"Something vibrant and fresh, with plenty of chime!"

The daisies join in with a cheerful shout,
While sunflowers sway, nearly losing the route.
"Keep it upbeat, we can't be too shy!"
Says the spicy little pepper, looking up to the sky.

A radish pipes up, trying hard to impress,
"What do you call sprouts that can dance? A mess!"
And with that, the choir erupts into song,
Celebrating their quirks, all winter long.

As they trill in the breeze, what a sight to behold,
Each melody sweet, each story retold.
From roots to the branches, in harmony's quest,
This funny green choir gave laughter its best!

Secrets of the Slow Unfolding

In the garden where whispers play,
A leaf giggles in the sun's warm ray,
The snails race with utmost pride,
While the daisies roll their eyes wide.

Mushrooms host a dance with flair,
Toadstools bounce without a care,
Earthworms wriggle, thinking they're cool,
While the daisies try to act like a fool.

Vines stretch out with tipsy grace,
They took a sip from a slug's embrace,
Who knew leaves could share such jokes,
With giggling bats and chuckling oaks?

So come, lend an ear to nature's jest,
In the chaos of bloom, we find our rest,
For life is a laugh, a frolicking spree,
In the garden where we roam wild and free.

The Language of Tender Growth

Little sprouts whisper, 'How do you do?',
As raindrops giggle and dance on the dew,
A sunflower winks with petals so bright,
'I'll steal the scene, just watch me take flight!'

The breeze carries secrets wrapped in leaf,
With roots that chuckle in comical grief,
Ah, how the daisies conspiringly scheme,
To outshine their neighbors, it's all in the dream!

A squirrel stops by with a nutty surprise,
While the daisies are striking their best pose and guise,
Each vine is a poet, each thorn has a tale,
While the blossoms giggle and tickle the gale.

So come to the patch where laughter resides,
Among petals and pollen where joy never hides,
In the world of green whispers and cheeky delight,
The language of growth is pure, nothing trite.

The Timeless Ballad of Greenery

In the meadow, grass sings a quirky tune,
While daisies dip low, under the moon,
Is that a frog croaking out a sweet rhyme?
Or just the wind bellowing, out of time?

The tree branches sway, with a cheeky grin,
While the worms in the dirt throw a party within,
What silliness creeps beneath thick, green cover,
Beneath the laughter, there's magic to discover!

Vines are the jesters, leaping on air,
Crafting a story with each twist and scare,
'Beware of the breeze!' they squeak with delight,
As petals all chuckle, holding on tight.

So let us rejoice in each bud's silly ploy,
As nature reveals her whimsical joy,
In the dance of the daisies and songs of the trees,
This timeless ballad flows sweet on the breeze.

The Unseen Tapestry of Life

In a garden where gossip thrives,
The petals talk, the gossip jives.
A carrot thinks it's quite profound,
While radish jokes go round and round.

The daisies laugh at passing bees,
They sway and dance with quirky knees.
A tomato winks, it's ripe with cheer,
While onions cry, they shed a tear.

The worms in soil wear tiny hats,
Debate in rhymes about their chats.
A sprout declares it's grown so tall,
While seedlings argue who's the small.

In the laughter of greens and blooms,
Life's absurdity always looms.
An echo of joy from roots so deep,
In nature's humor, secrets keep.

Whispers on the Wind

The breeze carries tales of yore,
As trees confide in roots galore.
A daffodil lifts its chin with pride,
"Who wore that hat? The squirrel!" it cried.

Old oak chuckles with a creaky voice,
"Got pranked by wind, it's not my choice!"
While ivy climbs without a care,
"Watch me scale—just grab a chair!"

A dandelion rustles with flair,
"I drift on air, just like my hair!"
While clouds above rush to and fro,
"Who needs a shower? Just watch us glow!"

In this laughter that flits and flies,
Nature's humor paints the skies.
With each gust, the world gets light,
As whispers twirl in sheer delight.

The Dialogue of Petals and Bark

Petals gossip, bark replies,
"Did you see that bird? No surprise!"
A rose quips, "I'm the fairest here!"
While daisies laugh, "Look, a deer!"

The trees roll branches, looking sly,
"Who wore those petals? Please comply!"
A lilac snickers, "What's the fuss?
At least we're not some silly plush!"

Sunflowers, tall, stuck in their ways,
"Just look at us in sunlit rays!"
But ferns retort with a cheeky grin,
"Cooler down here, it's where we win!"

In a laughter of colors and bark,
All comes alive, igniting spark.
As petals banter, a merry sight,
In nature's school, the fun ignites.

Legends Spun in Green

In shades of jade, stories unfold,
Lettuce whispers secrets bold.
A cucumber dreams of vast seas,
While carrots boast of ancient trees.

"Did you hear that tale?" asks a vine,
"Of veggies past—a life divine!"
A bean with swagger claims it's grand,
"Did you know I'm ruler of this land?"

The radish teases with a little flair,
"I'm the root of every dare!"
While corn cackles from heights so high,
"Look at me, I touch the sky!"

So in this garden, legends bloom,
As laughter echoes, filling the room.
In green we trust, with hearts so light,
Life's humorous tales dance in the night.

Chronicles of the Flourishing Fronds

In a garden lush and spry,
Fronds frolic, oh my my!
They giggle in the sunny breeze,
Making shadows dance with ease.

One frond wore a tiny hat,
Declared it looked quite fat.
Another said, "I'll wear a shoe!"
And off they went, a silly crew!

They twirled around a bumblebee,
Singing songs so cheerfully.
"Oh look, a tasty leaf to munch!"
But then they found it was a bunch!

The sun set low, the day grew dim,
But laughter still remained within.
As stars peeked down, they took a bow,
For fronds in laughter, they knew how!

Fables of the Wandering Vines

Vines wove tales of their great quest,
To find the root that looked the best.
One claimed it wore a shiny crown,
While others giggled, rolling down.

A twisty vine began to boast,
"I'm the best, so raise a toast!"
But all the others burst in cheer,
"You're just trying to persevere!"

They tangled up a hungry snail,
Who chewed on leaves without a trail.
"Excuse me sir, that's quite the bite,
But keep it down, the night's in sight!"

With everyone now laughing loud,
The moon peeked through a leafy shroud.
A tale of mischief, a vow to thrill,
For vines and friends, the fun won't chill!

Odes to the Connected Roots

Roots in secret, whisper low,
Sharing stories only they know.
One root chuckled, a pun so fine,
"I'm feeling grounded! Isn't that divine?"

Another chimed, "I dug so deep,
Found a treasure, and took a leap!"
But all the roots began to tease,
"You just found some worms, oh what a breeze!"

Together they'd stretch, reach it all,
Underground dance, a joyful sprawl.
With laughter echoing through the dirt,
They found their joy, no room for hurt.

As the soil hummed at night's embrace,
Connected roots found their own place.
In fun and friendship, they abide,
With whispers spreading far and wide!

Poetry of the Flourishing Canopy

In the canopy where giggles soar,
Leaves share secrets, laughter galore.
One spoke, "Look! My pet worm's a pet!"
While others laughed, "A worm? No bet!"

Branches swayed, a gentle tease,
With silly tales carried by the breeze.
One leaf slipped on a raindrop's path,
And the others roared, a hearty laugh!

"Why did the leaf cross the way?"
"To hang with the clouds and play all day!"
With antics bright, they skipped the gloom,
As sunlight filled their leafy room.

When nighttime came, stars on display,
They read their poems, night and day.
In joy of laughter, they found their tune,
Underneath the chuckling moon!

The Muse of Evergreen Shadows

In the garden, whispers sway,
Leaves giggle in a playful way.
They gossip about the sun's tease,
While dodging squirrels with such ease.

A raccoon dances, oh so spry,
Chasing shadows, he leaps high.
With every rustle, laughter grows,
Even the daisies strike a pose.

The breeze sings tunes of leafy jest,
Tickling branches, they don their best.
A matchup of chirps and chuckles too,
While petals drop, as if to boo.

In the realm where plants engage,
Nature's antics bloom on stage.
With playful roots that twist and turn,
They plot for fun—oh, how they yearn!

Refrains of a Hidden World

Among the ferns, a secret hum,
Tiny critters stealthy come.
In this orchestra of green delight,
Even the mushrooms wear a crown tight.

With googly eyes, the beetles stare,
Joining the chorus without a care.
The spiders swing on silken threads,
Jesting with ants inside their heads.

Under leaves, the shadows wink,
A world of laughter, don't you think?
With every flourish, chuckles arise,
As the sun peeks through the leafy guise.

In prickly thickets, jokes are spun,
Sunbeams join in, oh what fun!
Each rustle and whisper, a vibrant tune,
In the hidden world, all night till moon.

Patterns of Growth and Change

In the patch where wildflowers bloom,
With every sway, they dance and zoom.
Petals twirl, a colorful spree,
As bees crash in with glee—oh me!

Seeds hold secrets beneath the ground,
Waiting for sunbeams to come around.
Once shy sprouts now shout and prance,
In this festival of green romance.

The garden's humor grows with flair,
Leaves bow low and perform with care.
With a wink, they invite the rain,
As thunder chuckles, dancing again.

With every season, giggles flow,
From winter blank to summer's glow.
Change is just a playful game,
In nature's realm, who's to blame?

The Vignettes of the Twined Roots

Down below, where wonders twist,
Roots hold secrets, trails of mist.
Whispering tales of earth and rain,
They giggle softly, never mundane.

A pair of roots bump, then entangle,
In a dance that makes the squirrels wrangle.
Undergrowth parties, low and proud,
While moles and frogs cheer in the crowd.

With a flick, they trade their jests,
Roots drawing diagrams for tree quests.
In this tangled world, laughter wraps tight,
As evening stars twinkle, oh what a sight!

So if you listen, you might agree,
Nature's humor is wild and free.
In the depths, beneath our feet,
The roots continue, their jesters' beat.

Ethereal Notes from the Forest

In the woods where critters play,
A squirrel sings, hip-hip hooray!
A frog joins in with croaky cheer,
While birds chirp tunes that vanish near.

The trees all sway, they laugh and bend,
As branches sway and twist, they send,
A chorus of rustles, tickles, and sighs,
Echoing jokes 'neath bright blue skies.

The rabbits hop, they tap dance well,
Telling tales of acorn spells.
A hedgehog spins, it's quite a sight,
His spines aligned, oh what a fright!

The forest knows how to have fun,
Under the rays of a golden sun.
With giggles and puns, their spirits soar,
In this green theatre, there's always more!

The Symphonic Dance of Life

In gardens where the daisies jig,
A plucky bug does a little dig.
The ants all march in line so neat,
Choreographed to a tiny beat.

The roses sway with flowery grace,
While bees buzz by, they win the race.
They hum a tune, a sweet serenade,
Even the thorns join the parade!

The tomatoes blush, they giggle and bloom,
While pumpkins plot to dance in gloom.
A waltz of veggies on display,
Each veggie dreams of a grand ballet!

With vines that twist and leap for joy,
Nature's revelry, no need for a ploy.
A jolly gathering beneath the sun,
Where every laugh means the day is won!

The Essence of Interwoven Lives

With laughter knots and tangled threads,
A chatty plant shares what it spreads.
Vines whisper secrets, oh so sly,
As daisies wink and butterflies fly.

The twigs are gossiping, oh what fun,
About the clouds, the rain, the sun.
Lettuce giggles beneath the frail,
While carrots tell their tall-tale tale.

They weave a story, rich and grand,
A tapestry made by nature's hand.
Each petal and leaf joins the spree,
Creating a raucous symphony!

Rooted together, entwined in fate,
They dance through seasons, never late.
With humor bright, they spread their cheer,
In this wild garden, we hold so dear!

Brass and Ivy

There's a band of leaves with shining brass,
Each note they play makes the critters sass.
With froggy rhythms and crickets' chime,
They swing and sway, oh, what a time!

The ivy climbs with a jazzy flair,
Telling jokes, it fills the air.
A wobbly turtle taps his shell,
While the flowers' giggles ring like a bell.

Bees with trumpets buzz in delight,
As fireflies dance in the cool night.
Each flicker shines with playful jest,
Nature's concert is simply the best!

Together they play, a raucous delight,
Under the stars, a magical sight.
In this orchestral garden they thrive,
Making a melody that's fully alive!

www.ingramcontent.com/pod-product-compliance
Lightning Source LLC
Chambersburg PA
CBHW051634160426
43209CB00004B/643